THE WORLD'S GREATEST
SPACE VEHICLES

Ian Graham

Raintree

Chicago, Illinois

© Copyright 2006 Raintree
Published by Raintree,
a division of Reed Elsevier Inc.
Chicago, IL 60602

Customer Service 888-363-4266
Visit our website at
www.heinemannraintree.com

For more information address the publisher:
Raintree, 100 N. LaSalle, Suite 1200, Chicago,
IL 60602

Editorial: Andrew Farrow and Dan Nunn
Design: Ron Kamen and Philippa Baile
Picture Research: Hannah Taylor and Elaine
 Willis
Production: Duncan Gilbert

Originated by Dot Gradations Ltd.
Printed in China

The paper used to print this book comes from
sustainable resources.

10 09 08 07 06
10 9 8 7 6 5 4 3 2 1

**Library of Congress Cataloging-in-
Publication Data**
Graham, Ian, 1953-
  Space vehicles / Ian Graham.
    p. cm. -- (The world's greatest)
  Includes bibliographical references and
  index.
  ISBN 1-4109-2086-0 (library binding-
  hardcover) -- ISBN 1-4109-2093-3 (pbk.)
  1. Space vehicles--Juvenile literature.
  I. Title. II. Series.

  TL793.G6894 2005
  629.47--dc22

        2005016367

Acknowledgments
The publishers would like to thank the
following for permission to reproduce
photographs:

Associated Press pp. **14**, **15 bottom**; Corbis
pp. **5** (Roger Ressmeyer), **6** (Sygma), **7
bottom**, **10**, **11 bottom** (Reuters), **11
top** (Reuters/Sergei Karpukhin), **12**, **13 top**,
16 top (Roger Ressmeyer), **16 bottom**,
17 (Reuters), **19** (Reuters), **21 bottom**
(Reuters/NASA), **22**, **24**; NASA pp. **1** (SPEX),
4 (SPEX), **13 bottom**, **15 top**; Science Photo
Library pp. **7 top** (NASA), **8** (European Space
Agency), **9** (David Ducros), **20**, **21 top** (NASA),
23 (Detlev Van Ravenswaay).

Cover photograph of the U.S. Space Shuttle
Discovery taking off on October 29, 1998,
reproduced with permission of Getty Images.

Every effort has been made to contact
copyright holders of any material reproduced
in this book. Any omissions will be rectified in
subsequent printings if notice is given to the
publishers.

Contents

Some words are shown in bold, **like this**. You can find out what they mean by looking in the glossary.

Space Vehicles

The first space vehicle went into space in 1957. Now, lots of spaceflights are made every year. Most spacecraft fly around Earth, but some have been sent to the Moon and planets.

Getting off the ground

Space vehicles are launched by rockets. The biggest rockets are made from two or more pieces. These are called stages. When each stage has used up its fuel and is not needed any more, it falls away from the space vehicle.

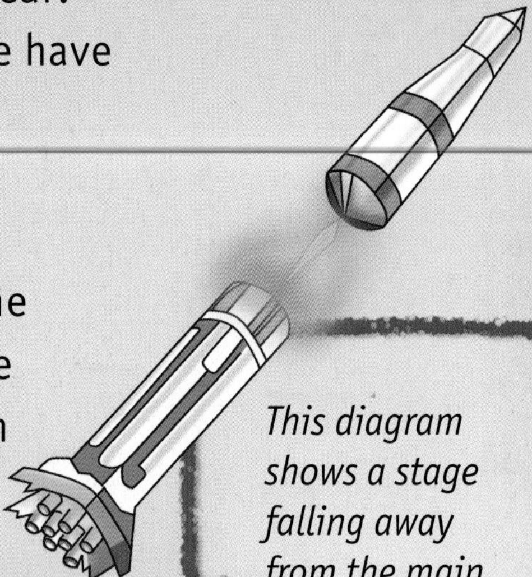

*This diagram shows a stage falling away from the main rocket as it blasts its way through the **atmosphere**.*

The rocket engines of the Space Shuttle power it into the sky on its way to space.

Fast fliers

Do you know how fast spacecraft fly? A spacecraft flying around Earth travels at 17,400 mph (28,000 kph). That's about 30 times faster than a jet airliner! Some spacecraft fly even faster. When the Apollo 10 spacecraft came back to Earth from a flight around the Moon, it reached nearly 25,000 mph (40,000 kph).

Unmanned **space probes** have been sent to all of the planets except Pluto, the furthest away.

The World's Greatest Space Mission

On July 16, 1969, three **astronauts** from the United States climbed into an Apollo spacecraft. They were Neil Armstrong, Edwin "Buzz" Aldrin, and Michael Collins. Four days later, Armstrong and Aldrin became the first people to walk on the Moon.

Setting course for the Moon

The Apollo spacecraft was launched by a giant rocket called the Saturn V (V means 5). The rocket put the spacecraft in **orbit** around Earth. When the spacecraft had been checked to make sure that everything was working properly, the rocket was fired again. This sent the spacecraft on its way to the Moon.

All the Apollo space missions to the Moon were launched by the Saturn V rocket. It never failed.

Apollo Moon-Landing Missions

Mission	Launched
Apollo 11	1969
Apollo 12	1969
Apollo 14	1971
Apollo 15	1971
Apollo 16	1972
Apollo 17	1972

There was also an Apollo 13 **mission**, but it was not able to land on the Moon because of an explosion in the spacecraft. The crew returned to Earth safely.

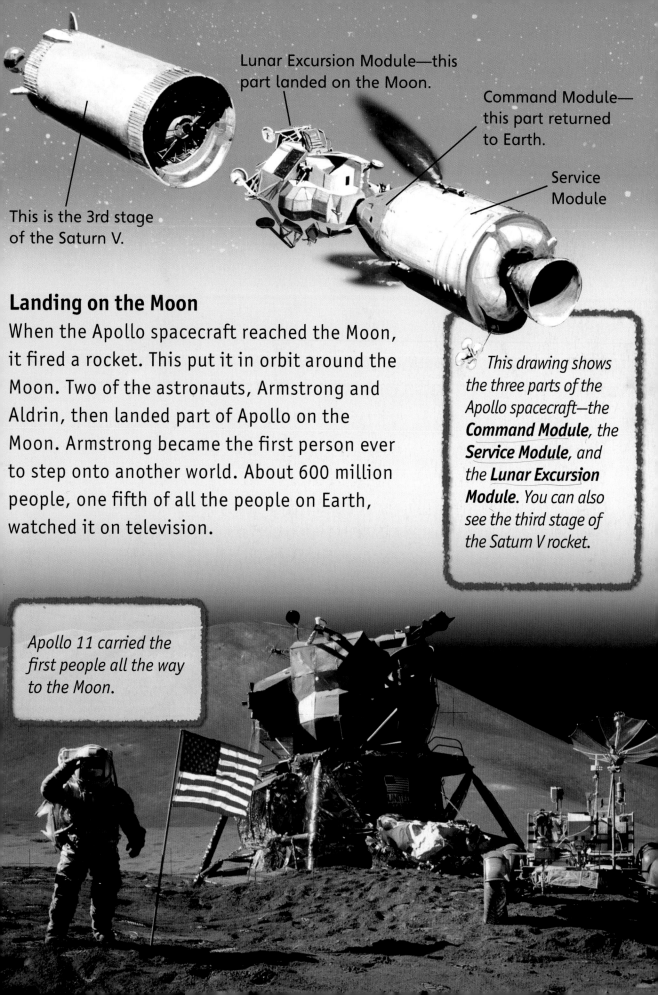

Lunar Excursion Module—this part landed on the Moon.

Command Module—this part returned to Earth.

Service Module

This is the 3rd stage of the Saturn V.

Landing on the Moon

When the Apollo spacecraft reached the Moon, it fired a rocket. This put it in orbit around the Moon. Two of the astronauts, Armstrong and Aldrin, then landed part of Apollo on the Moon. Armstrong became the first person ever to step onto another world. About 600 million people, one fifth of all the people on Earth, watched it on television.

This drawing shows the three parts of the Apollo spacecraft—the **Command Module**, the **Service Module**, and the **Lunar Excursion Module**. You can also see the third stage of the Saturn V rocket.

Apollo 11 carried the first people all the way to the Moon.

The Most Powerful Space Rockets

Europe's Ariane 5 rocket is one of the most powerful rockets for launching satellites today. Ariane 5 can launch satellites that weigh as much as seven or eight family cars to a great height above the Earth! The nose-cone at the top of the rocket can fit two large satellites inside. The satellites Ariane carries are also called its **payload**.

Ariane rockets are launched from a spaceport in South America. Most of the space inside an Ariane 5 launch rocket is filled with fuel.

Lift-off!

A main rocket and two boosters launch Ariane 5 into the sky. The boosters provide most of the force needed to lift Ariane off the launch-pad. They work for just over two minutes. Then they fall away. The main rocket carries on for another seven minutes or so. Then this falls away and a small upper rocket takes over. This rocket places the satellites in orbit around the Earth.

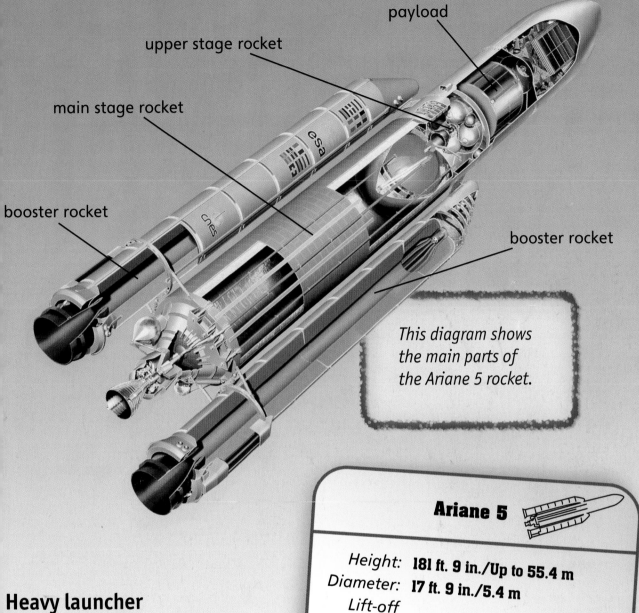

payload

upper stage rocket

main stage rocket

booster rocket

booster rocket

This diagram shows the main parts of the Ariane 5 rocket.

Heavy launcher

Russia's Proton rocket carries heavy payloads into a low orbit above the Earth. It launches satellites and parts of space stations. Proton rockets have been used since the 1960s.

Ariane 5

Height:	181 ft. 9 in./Up to 55.4 m
Diameter:	17 ft. 9 in./5.4 m
Lift-off Weight:	1,653,470 lb./Up to 750,000 kg
Maximum Payload:	35,275 lb./17.6 tons

HIGH FIVE
Ariane 5 is as tall as a 12-storey building.

The Most Successful Manned Space Vehicle

The Russian Soyuz spacecraft has been carrying people into space since 1967.

The Soyuz spacecraft

A Soyuz spacecraft has three main parts. The crew can live in two of them. The other part is full of fuel and instruments. The spacecraft has small rockets called **thrusters**. These are used to steer it in space. It also has **solar panels** to make electricity from sunlight.

solar panels

Descent Module

Orbital Module

docking port

Instrument Module

Cosmonauts *live and work in the Soyuz spacecraft's Orbital and Descent Modules.*

> When the Soyuz spacecraft returns to Earth, it uses a parachute to slow down before landing.

Space ferries

A Soyuz spacecraft can link up with other spacecraft. A door in the end of the Soyuz spacecraft opens when the spacecraft are connected. The crew can go through the door into the other spacecraft.

Soyuz craft carried crews to the Russian Salyut and Mir space stations. Today, they carry crews to the International Space Station. At the end of a mission, a crew returns to Earth. They travel in part of the spacecraft called the Descent **Module**. A heat shield on the front end protects the crew inside.

> A Soyuz spacecraft can carry a crew of one, two, or three.

Soyuz TMA spacecraft

Crew:	Up to 3
Length:	23 ft./7.0 m
Diameter:	9 ft./2.7 m
Span (across solar panels):	35 ft. 1 in./10.7 m
Weight:	15,915 lb./7,220 kg

11

The Most Reused Spacecraft

The U.S. Space Shuttle was the first space vehicle that could be used again and again, like an airliner. Space Shuttles have made more than 100 spaceflights since 1981.

The spaceplane

The Space Shuttle has four main parts. The astronauts fly inside the Orbiter. This is a spaceplane about the same size as a small airliner. A huge fuel tank and two rockets help it to take off. After launch, the empty fuel tank and booster rockets fall away. The Orbiter continues into space.

The Space Shuttle is launched into the sky by its engines and booster rockets.

Returning to Earth

The Orbiter is covered with special materials that protect it from heat. These are needed because the Orbiter heats up as it returns through the air to Earth. It gets so hot that it glows! The Orbiter then glides down to land on a runway at the Kennedy Space Center, located in Cape Canaveral, Florida.

The Space Shuttle can carry satellites and scientific instruments in its cargo bay.

Space Shuttle Orbiter

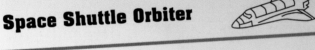

Crew: **2 pilots and up to 5 other astronauts**
Length: **122 ft./37.2 m**
Wingspan: **78 ft./23.8 m**
Weight: **218,960 lb./93,318 kg**
Orbit height: **Usually up to 248 mi./400 km above Earth**

The commander of the Orbiter lands it on a runway like an airliner.

The Biggest Space Station

Most manned spacecraft stay in space for a few weeks before they return to Earth. Space stations can stay in space for years.

The biggest space station is being built now. It is called the International Space Station, or ISS, because several countries are helping to build it. It is so big that it has to be launched in pieces. These are then put together in space. About 45 spaceflights will be needed to launch more than 100 pieces.

International Space Station

Crew:	**3 to 7**
Length:	**356 ft./108 m**
Width:	**290 ft./88 m**
Mass when finished:	**501.6 tons**
Height above Earth:	**249 mi./400 km**

The first part of the International Space Station was launched by a Russian rocket in 1998.

The space station grows bigger as more modules (pieces) are added. This picture shows it in 2004.

Going to work in space

United States Space Shuttles and Russian Soyuz spacecraft take astronauts to the ISS. They usually stay for about six months. They conduct science experiments and study Earth.

The International Space Station will be the biggest structure ever built in space. There will be more space inside than in the passenger cabin of a Boeing 747 Jumbo Jet.

Other Space Stations

The **Soviet Union** launched the first space station in 1971. It was the first of seven space stations called Salyut. The first Salyuts stayed in space for just a few months, but Salyut 7 (right) orbited Earth for nearly nine years.

Skylab

The United States launched its own space station in 1973. It was called Skylab. It was made from rockets and spacecraft that were not needed for the Apollo moon-landing missions. Three crews visited Skylab (below).

The Salyut 7 space station was launched in 1982.

*Skylab was shaken very hard while it was being launched. This shaking caused one of its two **solar panels** to break off.*

solar panel

Mir

The Soviet Union launched its Mir space station in 1986. Then extra modules were added to it to make it bigger. Mir stayed in space for 15 years.

Burning up

When all of these space stations reached the end of their working lives, they were left to fall into the atmosphere. As they fell, they broke up into pieces. The smallest pieces burned up, but the biggest pieces hit the ground or fell into the sea.

Mir Space Station

Module	Launched	Used for
Core Module	1986	control center and living area
Kvant-1	1987	studying stars
Kvant-2	1989	spacewalks
Kristall	1990	processing materials
Spektr	1995	studying the atmosphere
Priroda	1996	studying the oceans and atmosphere

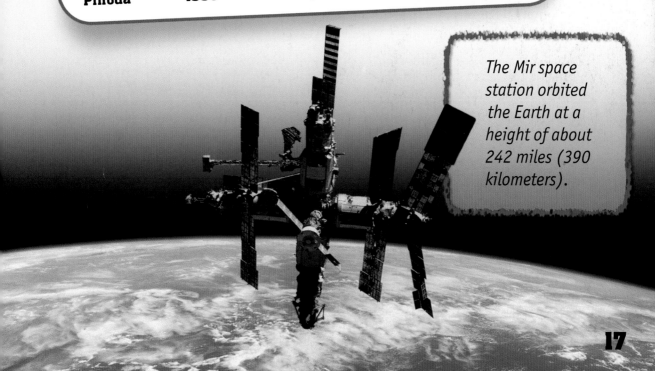

The Mir space station orbited the Earth at a height of about 242 miles (390 kilometers).

Amazing Spacecraft

No person has gone to other planets yet, but scientists have sent spacecraft to land on them. In 2004, two vehicles landed on Mars. They were called the Mars Exploration Rovers. One was nicknamed Spirit and the other one was called Opportunity.

1.

2.

3.

4.

5.

6.

7.

8

9

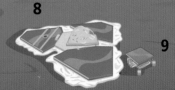

1. Space vehicle enters atmosphere.
2. Parachute pops out.
3. Heat shield falls away.
4. Air bags inflate.
5. Rockets fire to slow the lander.
6. Parachute is cut away.
7. Lander bounces on air bags.
8. Lander opens.
9. Mars Rover is ready to go.

This is how the Mars Exploration Rovers landed safely on the surface of Mars.

Looking for life

Mars is a dry, dusty planet. Scientists would like to
know if it had rivers and seas in the past. If there
was water on Mars, there may have been life, too.
There may even be some life on Mars today.

All in a day's work

The rovers study rocks. Their computers figure out
how to move around and do the work. When a rover
reaches a rock, it uses its instruments to find out
what the rock is made of.

*The Mars Exploration Rovers
have solar panels. These make
electricity for their cameras
and instruments.*

radio **antenna**

cameras

camera mast

radio antenna

solar panels

Other Amazing Spacecraf

Spirit and Opportunity were not the first amazing spacecraft to land on Mars. In 1976, two spacecraft called Viking landed on Mars. They measured the weather and they dug up some soil to test it. They also took lots of photographs of the planet's red surface. One lander worked for about four years. The other worked for about six years.

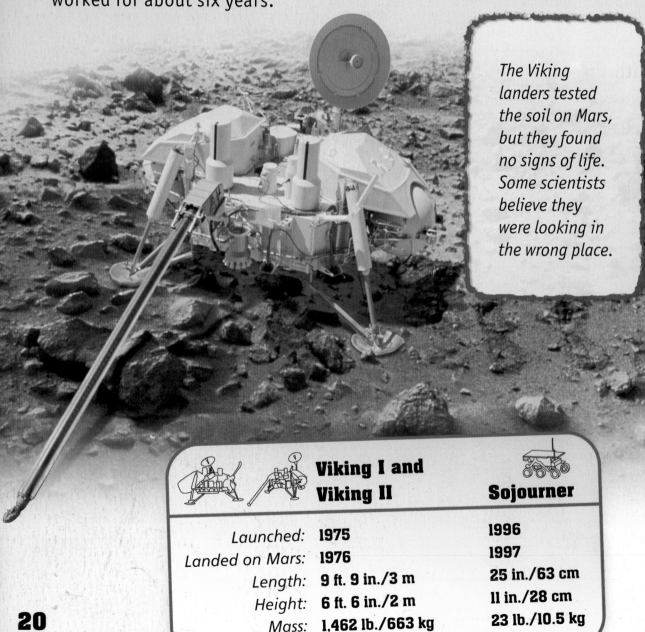

The Viking landers tested the soil on Mars, but they found no signs of life. Some scientists believe they were looking in the wrong place.

	Viking I and Viking II	Sojourner
Launched:	1975	1996
Landed on Mars:	1976	1997
Length:	9 ft. 9 in./3 m	25 in./63 cm
Height:	6 ft. 6 in./2 m	11 in./28 cm
Mass:	1,462 lb./663 kg	23 lb./10.5 kg

The solar panel on top of Sojourner produced electric power. This gave a top speed of about 16 inches (40 centimeters) per minute.

Driving on Mars

The Vikings could not move around, so in 1997, a small rover vehicle landed on Mars. It was called the Mars pathfinder rover, or Sojourner. It could go up to interesting rocks and study them with its instruments. A driver on Earth controlled Sojourner. Mars and Earth were so far apart that it took up to 15 minutes for commands to reach Sojourner. Sojourner kept working for nearly three months.

Scientists gave nicknames to the rocks studied by Sojourner. This rock was named Yogi.

25 in./63 cm

The Toughest Spacecraft

In 1985, the European Space Agency **(ESA)** sent a spacecraft to take close-up photographs of Halley's Comet. Comets look like fuzzy smudges with long bright tails. They are chunks of rock and ice that have been flying around the Sun for billions of years.

Most spacecraft would be destroyed if they flew through the dust around a comet. ESA had to make a supertough spacecraft for the job. The spacecraft was called Giotto.

Photographs from Giotto showed that Halley's Comet is a rock. It is about 9 miles (15 kilometers) long and 5 miles (8 kilometers) across.

Giotto flew into the dust around Halley's Comet at 155,000 mph (249,000 kph). Dust from Halley's Comet hit the Giotto spacecraft 50 times faster than a bullet!

comet dust   dust shield   solar panel   camera   dish radio antenna

Designing the dust buster

Giotto had a shield at the front to protect it from the comet's dust. The shield was made from two plates, one behind the other. Any dust that got through the front plate was caught by the plate behind it. A radio dish at the other end of the spacecraft sent photographs back to Earth.

What happened to Giotto?

Giotto was hit by dust from Halley's Comet 12,000 times, but it survived. It was then steered toward another comet, named Grigg-Skjellerup. Giotto arrived in 1992. Its camera had been destroyed by Halley's dust, but its other instruments took measurements. Then Giotto ran out of fuel, so it was left to drift in space.

The Most Widely Traveled Spacecraft

In the 1970s, the outer planets moved into a line across space. This was an amazing opportunity for a spacecraft to fly past nearly all of them, one after another. In 1977, two Voyager spacecraft were sent to study these planets.

The Voyager craft
The two Voyager spacecraft carried cameras and scientific instruments. They sent thousands of pictures and lots of other information back to Earth by radio.

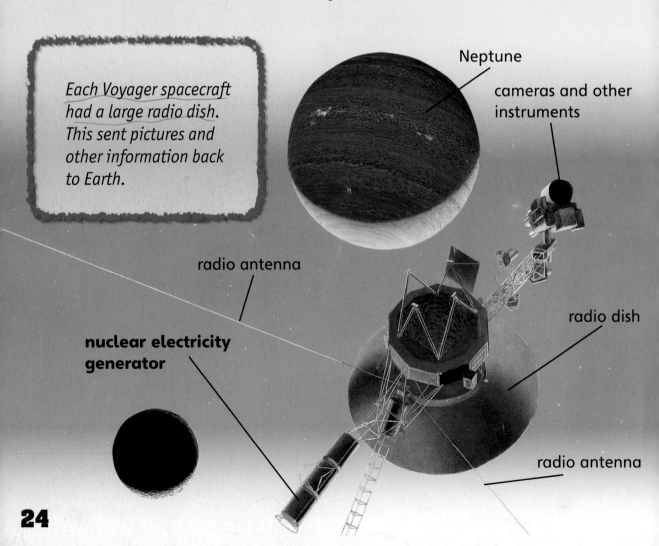

Each Voyager spacecraft had a large radio dish. This sent pictures and other information back to Earth.

Neptune

cameras and other instruments

radio antenna

radio dish

nuclear electricity generator

radio antenna

Still going

Both Voyagers are now heading out of the **solar system** toward the stars. They should keep working until about 2020. But which of them has traveled the furthest? The answer is Voyager 1. It is now about 9 billion miles (about 14.4 billion kilometers) away.

The Voyagers' Grand Tour

	Voyager 1	Voyager 2
Launched:	1977	1977
Jupiter:	1979	1979
Saturn:	1980	1981
Uranus:	–	1986
Neptune:	–	1989

Voyagers 1 and 2 took different paths through the solar system. Voyager 1 flew past Jupiter and Saturn. Voyager 2's flight path took it past four planets!

Each Voyager spacecraft was quite big—the dish alone was 12 feet 1 inch (3.7 meters) across.

24 ft. 7 in./7.5 m

Sun

Earth 93,000,000 miles from Sun

The distance from the Earth to the Sun is 93,000,000 miles. Follow the arrows to find out how far Voyager 1 has flown.

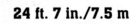

Facts and Figures

There have been dozens of space vehicles. Some of them are listed here. You can use the information to see which are the biggest and heaviest, which have made the most flights, which were built first and how many people they carried. Some rockets are made in lots of different versions. These are used for launching different spacecraft. Some of the figures change from mission to mission. If you want to know more about these or other space vehicles, see the section called Further Information on pages 30 and 31.

One-person Space Capsules	Height	Base Width	Mass	Manned Missions
Mercury (USA)	9.6 ft./2.9 m	6.2 ft./1.9 m	4,265 lb./1,935 kg	6 (1961–1963)
Vostok (USSR)	7 ft. 7 in./2.3 m	7 ft. 7 in./2.3 m	5,423 lb./2,460 kg	6 (1961–1963)

Two-person Space Capsules	Height	Base Width	Mass	Manned Missions
Gemini (USA)	18 ft. 5 in./5.6 m	10 ft./3.1 m	8,290 lb./3,760 kg	10 (1965–1966)

Three-person Spacecraft	Height	Base Width	Mass	Manned Missions
Apollo Command Module (USA)	10 ft. 7 in./3.2 m	12ft. 10 in./3.9 m	65,225 lb./29,600 /	15 (1968–1975)
Shenzhou (China)	28 ft. 5 in./8.65 m	9 ft. 2 in./2.8 m	17,200 lb./7,800 kg	1 (2003)
Soyuz (Russia)	23 ft./7.0 m	9 ft./2.7 m	15,915 lb./7,220 kg	more than 90*

* The Soyuz TMA spacecraft is still being used.

Spaceplanes	Length	Wingspan	Take-off Weight	Number Built
Buran (USSR)	119 ft. 4 in./36.37 m	78 ft. 6 in./23.92 m	165,000 lb./75,000 kg	1
Space Shuttle (USA)	122 ft./37.2 m	78 ft./23.8 m	218,960 lb./99,318 kg	6*

* including an Orbiter called Enterprise that has not gone into space

Space Stations	Launched	Mass	Time in Space	Fell Back to Earth
Skylab (USA)	1973	84.1 tons	6 years	1979
Salyut 7 (USSR)	1982	20.8 tons	9 years	1991
Mir (USSR)	1986	148.8 tons	15 years	2001
International Space Station	1998	501.6 tons	Still being built	Still in space

Satellites and Space Probes	Launched	Length or Diameter*	Mass	Planets Visited
Sputnik 1 (USSR)	1957	23 in./58 cm	185 lb./84 kg	Orbited Earth
Mariner 9 (USA)	1971	18 ft. 4 in./5.6 m	2,273 lb./1,031 kg	Orbited Mars
Pioneer 11 (USA)	1973	8 ft. 10 in./2.7 m	595 lb./270 kg	Flew past Jupiter and Saturn
Voyager 2 (USA)	1977	12 ft. 2 in./3.7 m	1,819 lb./825 kg	Flew past Jupiter, Saturn, Uranus, and Neptune
Magellan (USA)	1989	21 ft./6.4 m	7,593 lb./3,444 kg	Orbited Venus
Galileo (USA)	1989	29 ft. 6 in./9.0 m	8,556 lb./3,881 kg	Orbited Jupiter

* Satellites and space probes are different shapes, so it is difficult to give their sizes. These figures give an approximate comparison.

Landers	Launched	Length/Diameter	Mass	Landed
Luna 9 (USSR)	1966	24 in./60 cm	220 lb./100 kg	Moon, 1966
Venera 9 (USSR)	1975	7 ft. 11 in./2.4 m	3,440 lb./1,560 kg	Venus, 1975
Viking 1 & 2 (USA)	1975	9 ft. 9 in./3 m	1,462 lb./663 kg	Mars, 1976
Sojourner (USA)	1996	2 ft. 1 in./63 cm	23 lb./10.5 kg	Mars, 1997
Huygens (Europe)	1997	8 ft. 10 in./2.7 m	700 lb./318 kg	Titan (a moon of Saturn), 2005
Mars Exploration Rovers (USA)	2003	5 ft. 3 in./1.6 m	408 lb./185 kg	Mars, 2004

Rockets	When Used	Height	Mass	Used to launch
Vostok (USSR)	1960–1964	101 ft./30.8 m	620,325 lb./281,375 kg	Vostok spacecraft
Redstone-Mercury (USA)	1961	83 ft./25.3 m	66,000 lb./29,935 kg	Early Mercury spacecraft
Atlas-Mercury (USA)	1962–1963	92 ft. 10 in./28.3 m	366,985 lb./166,460 kg	Later Mercury spacecraft
Titan-Gemini (USA)	1964–1966	108 ft. 11 in./33.2 m	327,000 lb./148,325 kg	Gemini spacecraft
Saturn V (USA)	1967–1972	364 ft. 2 in./111 m	6,477,900 lb./2,938,312 kg	Apollo moon-landing spacecraft
Soyuz (USSR)	1966–today	151 ft. 3 in./46.1 m	672,410 lb./305,000 kg	Soyuz spacecraft
Proton (Russia)	1965–today	164 ft./50.0 m	1,529,590 lb./693,810 kg	Space Station parts and satellites
Energia-Buran (Russia)	1988	318 ft. 3 in./97.0 m	5,565,810 lb./2,524,600 kg	Buran spaceplane
Ariane 5 (Europe)	2002–today	181 ft. 9 in./55.4 m	1,653,470 lb./750,000 kg	Satellites

Glossary

antenna part of a radio that sends or receives radio waves. Radio antennae sometimes have metal dishes. These collect more radio waves or send them out in a stronger beam.

astronaut space traveler from the United States or Europe. Russian space travelers are called cosmonauts.

atmosphere the air or other gases around a planet

Command Module control center and living area of the Apollo spacecraft

cosmonaut Russian space traveler

ESA European Space Agency. It is the organization that manages non-military spaceflights for Europe.

Lunar Excursion Module (LEM) part of the Apollo spacecraft. It carried astronauts from orbit around the Moon down to the Moon's surface.

mission a task carried out by one or more astronauts or robot craft during a spaceflight

module part of a spacecraft, for example the Apollo spacecraft's Command Module

nuclear electricity generator device used by spacecraft to make electricity. It works by changing heat produced naturally by materials like uranium and plutonium into electricity.

orbit path of a spacecraft around a planet or moon. Also, the path of a moon around a planet, or a planet around the Sun.

payload equipment, astronauts, or satellites carried by a spacecraft

Service Module part of the Apollo spacecraft. It supplied the Command Module with water, electricity, gases, and rocket power.

solar panel sheet of solar cells on a spacecraft. These change sunlight into electricity. Spacecraft need electricity to power their cameras, instruments, and radio equipment.

solar system the Sun and everything that circles it—the nine planets, their moons, and all the other pieces of rock and ice that fly around the Sun

Soviet Union the group of countries led by Russia that launched the first satellite, the first manned spacecraft, and the first space station. Also known as the USSR.

space probe an unmanned spacecraft used to explore space

thruster small rocket or gas-jet that is fired to make small changes to a spacecraft's position

Voyager 1 has traveled 9,000,000,000 miles!

Voyager 1
9,000,000,000 miles

Further Information

You can find out more information about space, spaceflight, and space vehicles by reading the following books about these subjects.

Books to read

Bernards, Neal. *Mir Space Station (Above and Beyond)*. Mankato, Minnesota: Creative Education, 1999.

Herrod, Robin. *Space Shuttles (The History of Space Exploration)*. New York: World Almanac Library, 2004.

Nipaul, Devi. *The International Space Station: An Orbiting Laboratory*. Connecticut: Children's Press, 2004.

Spangengurg, Ray, and Kit and Diane Moser. *Onboard the Space Shuttle (Out of This World)*. New York: Franklin Watts, 2002.

Places to visit

The Kennedy Space Center
NASA's launch headquarters in Cape Canaveral, Florida allows you to experience what happens during a space shuttle launch. One tour takes you to see the International Space Station Center. Another tour features the first U.S. satellite and the rocket program of today.

National Air and Space Museum
There are two different Washington, D.C. locations of this museum: one on the National Mall and one near Dulles Airport called the Steven F. Udvar-Hazy Center.

The location on the mall features exhibits about the United States' journey to land on the Moon, as well as studies of the planets. The Udvar-Hazy Center features space-related artifacts. The Space Shuttle Enterprise is housed there for viewing.

Index